ZURI

TRAVEL GUIDE

Explore the Must-See Attractions in Switzerland's Metropolis

David A. Chris

Gratitude Page

Welcome to the Zurich Travel Guide! We are incredibly grateful that you've chosen our guide to accompany you on your journey through one of the world's most enchanting cities. Zurich, with its blend of historical charm and modern vibrancy, promises an experience like no other, and we are thrilled to be a part of your adventure.

Creating this guide has been a labor of love, and it would not have been possible without the support and contributions of many individuals and organizations. Our heartfelt thanks go out to the passionate locals who shared their insider tips and hidden gems, providing a unique and authentic perspective of Zurich. Their insights are the cornerstone of this guide, ensuring you experience the city as they do.

We extend our gratitude to the talented photographers and writers whose dedication to capturing Zurich's essence has enriched these pages with stunning visuals and captivating narratives. Their work brings the city's picturesque landscapes, vibrant neighborhoods, and cultural treasures to life, inspiring you to explore every corner.

Special thanks to the local businesses and attractions that offered their time and resources, making sure our information is accurate and up-to-date. Their commitment to excellence ensures that you, our valued reader, have the most rewarding and seamless experience possible.

Lastly, we are immensely grateful to you, our reader. Your trust and curiosity drive us to deliver the best travel guidance. We hope this guide helps you discover the magic of Zurich, creating memories that will last a lifetime.

We are grateful for having the opportunity to journey with you. Bon voyage!

Warmest regards,

The Zurich Travel Guide Team

Copyright © 2024 by David A. Chris
All rights reserved.

None of the parts of this book may be produced, kept in a recovering mechanism or transmitted in any way or by any method including electronics, mechanics, photocopying, recording and others without prior permission from the copyright owner.

Table of Contents

INTRODUCTION	**11**
CHAPTER 1	**16**
History and Culture of Zurich	16
Early Settlement and Colonial History	18
Geography and Topography	21
CHAPTER 2	**24**
Planning Your Trip	24
Best Time to Visit	24
Travel Documents and Visa Requirements	26
Budgeting Your Trip	27
Navigating Zurich	29
CHAPTER 3	**32**
Getting Around	32
By Air	32
By Bus	34
By Car & Motorcycle	34
By Boat	35
By Train	36
Hire or Renting Car/Boat	37
CHAPTER 4	**39**
Top Attractions	39
Lake Zurich (Zürichsee)	39
Old Town (Altstadt)	40

Swiss National Museum (Landesmuseum)	42
Bahnhofstrasse	43
Uetliberg Mountain	45
Kunsthaus Zurich	46
Zurich Zoo	48
Fraumünster Church	49
Lindenhof	50
Rietberg Museum	51
CHAPTER 5	**54**
Accommodation Options	54
Luxury Hotels	54
Mid-Range Hotels	56
Budget Accommodations	58
Hostels and Guesthouses	61
Unique Stays	63
Neighborhood Guide	65
Family-Friendly Locations	66
CHAPTER 6	**68**
Hidden Gems and Local Favorites	68
Off-the-Beaten-Path Neighborhoods	68
Unique Cafes	70
Unique Restaurants	72
CHAPTER 7	**74**
Cultural Experiences	74
Museums and Galleries	74
Performing Arts	76

Local Festivals	77
CHAPTER 8	**80**
Outdoor Activities	80
Hiking and Walking Trails	80
Biking Routes	81
Water Sports on Lake Zurich	82
Winter Sports	83
Ice Skating Rinks	84
Parks and Gardens	85
CHAPTER 9	**87**
Day Trips and Excursions	87
Lucerne	87
Rhine Falls	88
Mount Titlis	89
Rapperswil-Jona	90
Appenzell and Ebenalp	91
Winterthur	92
CHAPTER 10	**94**
Shopping	94
Popular Shopping Districts	94
Independent Boutiques and Local Designers	96
Souvenirs and Swiss Specialties	97
Shopping Malls and Department Stores	97
Flea Markets and Vintage Shops	98
CHAPTER 11	**100**
Practical Information	100

Language Tips	100
Emergency Contacts	101
Local Etiquette and Customs	101
Electricity and Plug Types	102
Health and Safety	102
Internet and SIM Cards	103
Accessibility Information	103
Public Holidays	104
Money Matters	104
Tipping	105
Dos and Don'ts	105
7-Day Itinerary for Zurich	**107**
CONCLUSION	**114**

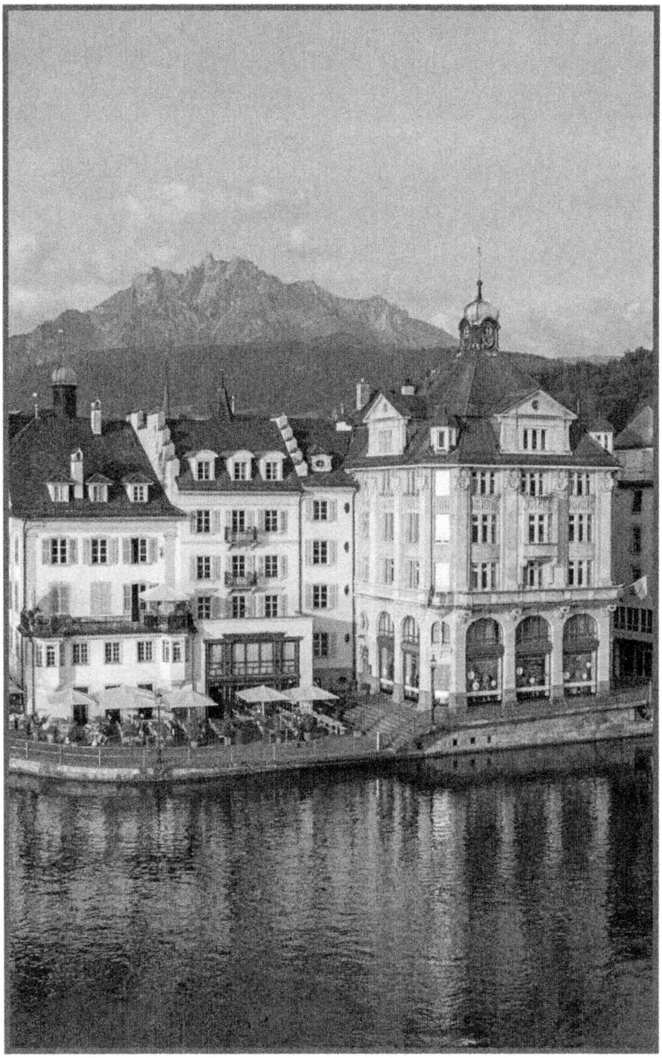

ZURICH

[Map of Zürich showing locations including Zürich - Hauptbahnhof, Bäckerei-Konditorei Stocker, Zürich Bahnhofplatz/HB, Bahnhofquai/HB, Central Plaza (4.2 ★ (845), 4-star hotel), Weber by store, Züri Bistro, Laderach, McDonald's, UBS Polybahn (Funicular railway to ETH Zürich campus), Central, Ruby Mimi Hotel & Bar, Beatenpl, Rhein, Hilti Dachterrasse Vegetarian · $$, Mühlesteg]

SCAN THE QR CODE

1. Open your device's camera app.
2. Point the camera at the QR code.
3. Ensure the QR code is within the frame and well-lit.
4. Wait for your device to recognize the QR code.
5. Once recognized, tap on the notification or follow the prompt to access the content or action associated with the QR code.

INTRODUCTION

Welcome to Zurich, a city that beautifully marries the old and the new, offering a unique blend of history, culture, and modernity. As an avid traveler and dedicated travel guide author, I am thrilled to present to you this comprehensive guide to one of Europe's most captivating destinations. My name is David A. Chris, and my journey with Zurich began over a decade ago, during a serendipitous backpacking trip across Europe. Zurich instantly captivated me with its charm, and since then, I have made numerous visits, each time uncovering new facets of this remarkable city.

With a background in history and a passion for storytelling, I have spent the last 15 years exploring cities across the globe, writing travel guides that delve deep into the heart and soul of each destination. Zurich, however, holds a special place in my heart. Its picturesque landscapes, rich cultural tapestry, and dynamic lifestyle make it a city worth exploring again and again. In this guide, I aim to share my extensive knowledge and experiences, providing you with an insider's view of Zurich, ensuring you have a memorable and enriching visit.

Why Choose This Guide?
When it comes to planning your trip, having a reliable and detailed guidebook is crucial. This Zurich Travel Guide is designed to be your ultimate companion, offering comprehensive insights and practical advice that cater to all types of travelers. Whether you are a history buff, a foodie, an art enthusiast, or simply someone looking to relax and enjoy the scenic beauty, this guide has something for everyone.

In this book, you will find meticulously researched information on Zurich's top attractions, hidden gems, local customs, and practical tips to navigate the city effortlessly. I have personally visited each recommended spot, ensuring that you get firsthand, authentic information. Additionally, the guide includes maps, suggested itineraries, and budget tips, making it a one-stop resource for all your travel needs.

Religion and Culture
Zurich is a melting pot of cultures, where traditional Swiss values coexist harmoniously with modern, cosmopolitan influences. The predominant religion here is Christianity, with a majority of the population identifying as Protestant or Catholic. However, the city is also home to a diverse community of people from various religious

backgrounds, including Islam, Judaism, and Buddhism. This diversity is reflected in Zurich's vibrant cultural scene, which boasts an array of festivals, art exhibitions, and culinary experiences.

One of the most captivating aspects of Zurich's culture is its deep-rooted tradition of hospitality and punctuality. The Swiss are known for their politeness and efficiency, which you will undoubtedly experience during your stay. The city's cultural calendar is packed with events, from the lively Street Parade to the traditional Sechseläuten, offering you a chance to immerse yourself in local customs and celebrations.

A Brief History of Zurich
Zurich's history dates back over 2,000 years, with its origins as a Roman customs post called Turicum. Throughout the centuries, Zurich evolved into a significant center for trade, education, and finance. In the 16th century, it played a pivotal role in the Protestant Reformation under the leadership of Huldrych Zwingli, a legacy that continues to shape its religious and cultural landscape today.

The city's historical significance is demonstrated by its well-preserved architecture and various museums. The Old Town, with its narrow, winding streets and medieval buildings, offers a glimpse into

Zurich's storied past, while institutions like the Swiss National Museum provide a deeper understanding of its historical and cultural evolution.

Currency and Laws
Switzerland is known for its strong financial system, and Zurich, as its financial hub, operates with the Swiss Franc (CHF) as the official currency. While credit cards are widely accepted, it is advisable to carry some cash for smaller establishments and public transportation. ATMs are plentiful, and currency exchange services are readily available.

When it comes to laws, Switzerland is renowned for its strict regulations and emphasis on orderliness. Smoking is prohibited in enclosed public spaces, including restaurants and bars, although designated smoking areas are available. It's important to note that Switzerland has stringent drug laws, and even small quantities of illegal substances can result in severe penalties. Additionally, always remember to carry your identification, as spot checks by the police are not uncommon.

This guide will take you through Zurich's iconic landmarks, such as the majestic Grossmünster and the serene Lake Zurich, as well as off-the-beaten-path treasures like hidden courtyards and charming neighborhood cafes. You'll discover the best spots to savor Swiss delicacies, from fondue and raclette to artisanal chocolates, and explore bustling markets and chic boutiques that showcase the city's unique style.

For art and history enthusiasts, Zurich offers a wealth of museums and galleries, including the renowned Kunsthaus Zurich and the historic Lindenhof. Nature lovers will appreciate the city's numerous parks and proximity to the Swiss Alps, providing ample opportunities for hiking, skiing, and other outdoor adventures.

In creating this Zurich Travel Guide, my goal is to provide you with a resource that is both informative and inspiring. Whether it's your first visit or you're returning to rediscover this incredible city, I hope this guide helps you make the most of your time in Zurich. Thank you for choosing this book as your travel companion. Here's to unforgettable adventures and cherished memories in the heart of Switzerland.

CHAPTER 1

History and Culture of Zurich

Zurich, Switzerland's largest city and economic powerhouse, is a captivating blend of historical charm and contemporary sophistication. Nestled along the banks of the Limmat River and the shores of Lake Zurich, this vibrant metropolis offers stunning natural landscapes, a rich cultural heritage, and a high quality of life. With its well-preserved medieval Old Town, world-class museums, and dynamic arts scene, Zurich stands as a testament to Switzerland's enduring legacy of innovation, culture, and tradition.

Culture of Zurich

Zurich's culture is a rich tapestry woven from its historical roots, diverse population, and modern influences. The city is predominantly Christian, with Protestant and Catholic communities playing significant roles. However, Zurich is also home to a vibrant mix of cultures and religions, including Islam, Judaism, Buddhism, and Hinduism, reflecting its cosmopolitan character.

The city's cultural scene is dynamic and varied, offering a plethora of museums, galleries, theaters, and music venues. The Kunsthaus Zurich, Swiss

National Museum, and Rietberg Museum are just a few of the institutions that showcase the city's artistic and historical treasures. Zurich's performing arts scene is equally impressive, with the Zurich Opera House and Schauspielhaus Zurich hosting world-class productions.

Festivals and events are integral to Zurich's cultural fabric. The Zurich Film Festival, Street Parade, and Sechseläuten are some of the major events that draw locals and tourists alike, celebrating everything from cinematic excellence to electronic music and traditional spring rituals.

Culinary traditions in Zurich reflect both Swiss heritage and international influences. From indulging in fondue and raclette to exploring a plethora of global cuisines, Zurich's food scene caters to all tastes. The city's markets, like the bustling Viadukt Market, offer fresh, local produce and artisanal products, highlighting the importance of quality and sustainability in Zurich's culinary culture.

Zurich's history and culture are integral to understanding its identity as a city. Its journey from a Roman settlement to a modern global hub is marked by resilience, innovation, and a deep appreciation for tradition and progress. As you explore Zurich, you'll discover a city that cherishes its past while embracing the future, offering a rich and rewarding experience for every visitor.

Early Settlement and Colonial History

Zurich's history dates back over 2,000 years. The earliest settlements in the area were established during the Neolithic period, with evidence of human activity found on Lindenhof Hill, a site that remains significant today. The Romans arrived around 15 BC, establishing a customs station called Turicum, which served as a strategic location along important trade routes. Over time, this settlement evolved into a thriving market town.

During the early medieval period, Zurich continued to grow under the rule of the Alemanni, a Germanic tribe. By the 9th century, it became a royal residence of the Carolingian dynasty, which further solidified its status as an important regional center. The foundation of the Fraumünster Abbey in 853 by King Louis the German marked a significant moment, as the abbey wielded considerable power and influence over the city's development.

The Middle Ages
The Middle Ages were a transformative period for Zurich. In 1218, the city gained the status of an imperial free city, which allowed it greater autonomy and economic freedom. This newfound independence spurred growth and prosperity, leading to the construction of key architectural landmarks such as the Grossmünster, a Romanesque-style Protestant church that remains an iconic symbol of Zurich.

During this time, Zurich became a member of the Swiss Confederation in 1351, aligning itself with neighboring cantons to enhance mutual defense and economic cooperation. This alliance was crucial in establishing Zurich as a significant political and economic player in the region. The city's thriving textile industry, particularly in silk production, contributed to its wealth and influence.

The 16th and 17th Centuries
The 16th century marked a pivotal era in Zurich's history with the onset of the Protestant Reformation. Huldrych Zwingli, a leading figure of the Reformation, began his influential preaching at the Grossmünster in 1519. His ideas quickly spread, and Zurich became a stronghold of Protestantism, leading to significant religious, social, and political changes. The city's adoption of Protestantism also

resulted in the dissolution of monasteries and the secularization of church properties.

The 17th century saw Zurich continue to thrive as a center of trade and commerce. The city's strategic location at the crossroads of major European trade routes facilitated the exchange of goods, ideas, and culture. During this period, Zurich also established itself as a hub of education and learning, with the founding of institutions that would later evolve into the University of Zurich.

The 18th to 20th Century
The 18th century ushered in the Enlightenment, and Zurich embraced new ideas in science, philosophy, and the arts. The city became a magnet for intellectuals, artists, and writers. Johann Heinrich Pestalozzi, a pioneer in education, and Johann Jakob Bodmer, a prominent literary figure, were among the notable individuals who contributed to Zurich's intellectual and cultural landscape.

The 19th century brought industrialization, transforming Zurich into a modern city. The construction of the Swiss Federal Railways and the opening of the Gotthard Railway Tunnel in the late 1800s enhanced Zurich's connectivity and economic growth. The city's population boomed, and it became a leading financial center, with the establishment of major banks and insurance companies.

World War II and Post-War Decades

During World War II, Switzerland maintained a policy of neutrality, and Zurich, like the rest of the country, remained unscathed by direct conflict. However, the city played a crucial role as a center for espionage and diplomacy. Zurich's financial institutions became a safe haven for assets, and the city's international connections facilitated discreet negotiations and intelligence activities.

In the post-war decades, Zurich experienced rapid modernization and expansion. The city's skyline evolved with the construction of modern buildings and infrastructure. Zurich's financial sector continued to grow, solidifying its reputation as a global financial hub. The city also became known for its high quality of life, attracting people from around the world to live, work, and study.

Geography and Topography

Zurich is located in the heart of Switzerland, straddling the Limmat River where it flows out of Lake Zurich. The city is surrounded by rolling hills and is characterized by its picturesque natural setting. The Uetliberg Mountain, standing to the southwest, offers panoramic views of the city and the lake. Zurich's strategic location has historically made it a crossroads for trade and travel, enhancing its cultural and economic significance.

Key Historical Events
- Roman Settlement (15 BC): Establishment of Turicum, a Roman customs station.
- Foundation of Fraumünster Abbey (853): Significant religious and political influence.
- Imperial Free City Status (1218): Gained autonomy and economic freedom.
- Swiss Confederation Membership (1351): Strengthened political and economic alliances.
- Protestant Reformation (1519): Led by Huldrych Zwingli, transforming religious and social structures.
- Industrialization (19th Century): Rapid growth and modernization, becoming a financial center.
- World War II: Maintained neutrality, became a center for espionage and diplomacy.

In this guide, I aim to provide you with an in-depth understanding of Zurich's history and culture, helping you appreciate the unique charm and significance of this remarkable city. From its early settlements to its vibrant present, Zurich's story is one of continuous transformation and enduring allure. Welcome to Zurich, and may your journey through its history and culture be as enriching as it is enjoyable.

CHAPTER 2

Planning Your Trip

Zurich, the largest city in Switzerland, is a vibrant and picturesque destination that seamlessly blends modernity with rich history. Whether you're drawn by its world-class museums, vibrant nightlife, serene lakeside, or proximity to the Swiss Alps, Zurich has something to offer every traveler. Planning ahead of time will help you make the most of your trip.

Best Time to Visit

Zurich's climate is temperate with four distinct seasons:

Spring (March to May): Spring in Zurich is a beautiful time to visit. As the snow melts and flowers bloom, the city comes alive with colors. Temperatures vary between 5°C and 15°C (41°F to 59°F). This is an excellent time for outdoor activities and sightseeing without the summer crowds.

Summer (June to August): Summer is peak tourist season, with temperatures averaging between 15°C to 25°C (59°F to 77°F). The warm weather is perfect for swimming in Lake Zurich, hiking in nearby mountains, and enjoying open-air festivals. However, be prepared for larger numbers and higher pricing.

Autumn (September to November): Fall brings cooler temperatures (10°C to 15°C or 50°F to 59°F) and fewer tourists. The autumn foliage gives a lovely appeal to the city. It's an ideal time for cultural visits and exploring Zurich's numerous museums and galleries.

Winter (December to February): Winter is cold, with temperatures ranging from -2°C to 5°C (28°F to 41°F). While it's not as busy as the summer, Zurich is a gateway to excellent skiing in the nearby Alps. The city itself transforms into a winter wonderland, particularly during the festive Christmas season.

Major Events and Festivals
Zurich hosts a variety of events throughout the year, catering to diverse interests:

Zurich Film Festival (September): This festival attracts filmmakers and cinema enthusiasts from around the globe. It showcases new talent and high-profile premieres in a lively atmosphere.

Street Parade (August): One of the world's largest techno parties, the Street Parade is a vibrant, colorful event that takes over the streets of Zurich with music, dancing, and elaborate costumes.

Sechseläuten (April): This traditional spring festival involves a parade of guilds, the burning of the Böögg (a snowman effigy), and various cultural festivities, marking the end of winter.

Zurich Christmas Markets (December): Zurich transforms into a magical winter wonderland with Christmas markets spread across the city, featuring festive decorations, delicious treats, and unique gifts.

Travel Documents and Visa Requirements

Before traveling to Zurich, ensure you have the necessary travel documents. Switzerland is part of the Schengen Area, which means visitors from Schengen countries do not need a visa for stays of up to 90 days.

- EU/EEA Nationals: Only a valid passport or ID card is required for entry.

- Non-EU/EEA Nationals: You may need a Schengen visa, depending on your country of origin. Check with the Swiss embassy or consulate in your home country for specific requirements.

You must ensure that your passport is valid for a minimum of three months beyond the date you intend to travel from the Schengen Area. Always check the latest entry requirements before your trip, as regulations can change.

Budgeting Your Trip

Zurich is known for its high standard of living, which can translate to higher travel costs. However, with careful planning, you can manage your budget effectively.

Cost Estimates
- Accommodation: Budget options like hostels and guesthouses start at CHF 50-80 per night. Mid-range hotels range from CHF 100-250, while luxury hotels can exceed CHF 400 per night.
- Food: Dining out can be expensive, with a typical meal at a mid-range restaurant costing CHF 25-50. Cheaper options like takeaways, bakeries, and grocery stores can

help you save money. Budget around CHF 20-40 per day if you're eating on a budget.
- Transportation: A Zurich Card, which offers unlimited travel on public transportation and free or reduced admission to many attractions, costs CHF 27 for 24 hours or CHF 53 for 72 hours.
- Attractions: Entry fees for museums and attractions vary, typically ranging from CHF 10-20. Many outdoor activities, such as hiking and swimming in Lake Zurich, are free.

Money-Saving Tips
- Zurich Card: This card is a great investment, offering unlimited travel on public transport and discounts on many attractions.
- Free Activities: Take advantage of free walking tours, parks, and lakeside promenades.
- Eat Like a Local: Visit local markets, bakeries, and grocery stores for affordable meals. Try the budget-friendly lunch menus (Mittagsmenüs) available at many restaurants.
- Accommodation: Consider staying in budget-friendly hostels, guesthouses, or Airbnb rentals.

Navigating Zurich

Getting around Zurich is easy and efficient, thanks to its excellent public transportation system.

Public Transportation
Zurich boasts an extensive and reliable public transport network, including trams, buses, trains, and boats:

- Trams and Buses: The tram and bus networks cover the entire city and are the most convenient way to travel. They operate frequently, and the Zurich Card provides unlimited travel.
- Trains: Zurich's main train station, Zürich Hauptbahnhof (HB), is a central hub for local, regional, and international trains. The Swiss Federal Railways (SBB) provides efficient services throughout Switzerland.
- Boats: Enjoy a scenic boat ride on Lake Zurich or along the Limmat River. These are included with the Zurich Card.

Car Rentals and Driving
While Zurich has a superb public transport system, you might consider renting a car if you plan to explore the surrounding regions or the Swiss Alps:

- Car Rentals: Major car rental companies operate in Zurich, and you can pick up a car at the airport or various city locations. Remember that parking in Zurich can be expensive and challenging.
- Driving Tips: Switzerland has an excellent road network, but be aware of strict traffic regulations. Speed limits are strictly enforced, and it's mandatory to have a highway vignette (toll sticker) for using Swiss motorways.

Biking and Walking

Zurich is a bike-friendly city with numerous cycling paths and bike rental services. Exploring the city by bike can be enjoyable, especially in good weather. Zurich also has several pedestrian zones, making walking a pleasant and practical option for shorter distances.

- Bike Rentals: Services like Züri Rollt offer free bike rentals for a refundable deposit. Additionally, you can find a number of private bike rental services.
- Walking: Many of Zurich's attractions are within walking distance of each other. The Old Town (Altstadt), with its narrow streets and historical buildings, is best explored on foot.

Zurich is a dynamic city offering a mix of cultural experiences, outdoor activities, and scenic beauty. With careful planning, you can make the most of your visit, regardless of your budget. From its efficient public transportation system to its rich calendar of events and festivals, Zurich welcomes travelers with open arms and promises an unforgettable experience.

CHAPTER 3

Getting Around

Zurich, a bustling metropolis nestled by Lake Zurich, offers a range of transportation options to suit every traveler. Whether you're arriving by air, bus, car, or boat, Zurich's efficient and well-organized transit systems ensure a smooth journey. Here's a comprehensive guide to navigating Zurich.

By Air

Zurich Airport (ZRH), also known as Kloten Airport, is Switzerland's largest international airport, located approximately 10 kilometers (6 miles) north of the city center. It is a major hub for Swiss International Air Lines and connects Zurich to destinations worldwide.

Transportation from Zurich Airport
Train
The fastest way to get to the city center is via rail. The SBB (Swiss Federal Railways) operates frequent trains from Zurich Airport to Zurich Main Train Station (HB). Trains run every 5-10 minutes, and the journey takes about 10-15 minutes. A single

ticket costs CHF 6.80 for adults and CHF 3.40 for children (6-16 years).

Tram
The Glattalbahn tram line (number 10) connects Zurich Airport to the city center. The tram journey takes about 35 minutes, offering a scenic route through Zurich's suburbs. A single ticket costs CHF 6.80.

Taxi
Taxis are available outside the arrivals terminal. The ride to the city center takes around 20-30 minutes, depending on traffic, and costs approximately CHF 50-70.

Shuttle Services
Several hotels provide transportation to and from the airport. There are also shared shuttle services available, which are a cost-effective option if you have light luggage and don't mind a few extra stops. Prices vary by provider but generally range from CHF 25-35 per person.

Destinations from Zurich Airport
From Zurich Airport, you can easily access various Swiss cities and neighboring countries. Major train routes connect Zurich to cities like Geneva, Basel,

Bern, and Lausanne, as well as international destinations such as Milan, Munich, and Paris.

By Bus

Zurich's bus network is extensive and well-integrated with the tram and train systems. Buses are a reliable and convenient option for getting around the city and its suburbs.

Key Information
- Frequency: Buses run frequently, especially during peak hours. Most routes operate from early morning until midnight.
- Tickets: Tickets are valid across trams, buses, and local trains. A single ticket within Zurich's central zones (Zone 110) costs CHF 4.40 and is valid for 1 hour. Day passes are also available for CHF 8.80, offering unlimited travel within the specified zones.
- Night Buses: Zurich operates a night bus service on weekends, ensuring safe travel even in the late hours.

By Car & Motorcycle

Major Highways
Zurich is well-connected by a network of major highways:

- A1: Connects Zurich to Geneva and St. Gallen.
- A3: Runs from Zurich to Chur and connects to the A13 towards Italy.
- A4: Links Zurich to the north, leading to Germany.

Parking in Zurich

Parking in Zurich can be challenging and expensive:
- On-Street Parking: Limited and metered, costing around CHF 1.50-2.00 per hour.
- Parking Garages: Numerous parking garages are available throughout the city, charging approximately CHF 3-4 per hour or CHF 35-50 for a full day.
- Park & Ride: Located on the outskirts, these facilities allow you to park your car and use public transport to reach the city center. Prices are lower, at around CHF 15-20 per day.

By Boat

Zurich's location by Lake Zurich and the Limmat River makes boat travel a scenic and enjoyable option.

Key Routes
- Lake Zurich Boats: Operates year-round, offering regular services between Zurich and towns along the lake, such as Rapperswil. A round trip from Zurich to Rapperswil costs around CHF 26.
- Limmat River Boats: Operates from April to October, navigating the Limmat River from Lake Zurich to the Landesmuseum. A single journey costs CHF 4.40.

Private Boat Hire
You can also hire private boats for personal excursions. Prices vary based on the type and size of the boat:
- Rowboats and Paddle Boats: Start at CHF 20 per hour.
- Motorboats: Range from CHF 60-100 per hour.
- Luxury Yacht Charters: Can cost upwards of CHF 300 per hour.

By Train

Zurich Main Train Station (HB)
Zurich Hauptbahnhof (HB) is one of Europe's busiest railway stations, serving as a central hub for national and international trains.

Major Train Routes
- Domestic: Frequent connections to Geneva (2h 45m), Basel (1h), Bern (1h), and Lucerne (45m). Tickets range from CHF 25-80 depending on the destination and class.
- International: Direct trains to cities like Milan (3h 30m, starting at CHF 90), Munich (4h, starting at CHF 60), and Paris (4h 15m, starting at CHF 120).

Facilities and Services
Zurich HB offers a range of amenities:
- Shopping: Numerous shops, from fashion to groceries, are open seven days a week.
- Dining: A variety of restaurants and cafes cater to all tastes and budgets.
- Luggage Services: Lockers and luggage transport services are available.
- Tourist Information: A tourist information center provides maps, tickets, and advice.

Hire or Renting Car/Boat
Car Rental
Major car rental companies operate in Zurich, including Avis, Hertz, and Europcar. Prices for a standard car rental start at around CHF 60-80 per

day. For long-term rentals, weekly rates can range from CHF 350-500.

Boat Rental

Boat rental options range from simple rowboats to luxurious yachts:
- Row Boats/Paddle Boats: CHF 20 per hour.
- Motorboats: CHF 60-100 per hour.
- Luxury Yachts: CHF 300-500 per hour, with possible additional charges for a skipper and fuel.

Navigating Zurich is straightforward, thanks to its well-developed transportation infrastructure. Whether you prefer the efficiency of public transport, the freedom of a rental car, or the scenic routes by boat, Zurich offers a variety of options to suit your travel style and budget. With this guide, you're well-equipped to explore Zurich and its stunning surroundings effortlessly.

CHAPTER 4

Top Attractions

Zurich, Switzerland's largest city, is renowned for its beautiful landscapes, rich history, and vibrant cultural scene. Here's a guide to the top 10 attractions in Zurich, complete with historical backgrounds, practical information, and tips for making the most of your visit.

Lake Zurich (Zürichsee)

Lake Zurich has been a central part of the city since Roman times, serving as a vital trade route. Over the centuries, it has evolved into a recreational hotspot.

Opening Hours
Open 24/7

Admission Fees
Free

Address & Location
Lake Zurich, Zurich, Switzerland

Getting There
- By Train: S-Bahn to Zürich Stadelhofen

- By Tram: Lines 2, 4 to Bellevue

Why Visit
Tourists flock to Lake Zurich for its stunning scenery, boating, and relaxing promenades. The lake offers a tranquil escape with picturesque views of the Alps.

Outdoor Activities
- Boating
- Swimming
- Picnicking
- Walking and cycling paths

Pro Tips
- Visit during the evening for spectacular sunset views.
- Rent a paddleboat for a fun experience on the lake.

Don't Miss
- The Chinese Garden
- Quaibrücke bridge for panoramic views

Old Town (Altstadt)

Zurich's Old Town is a charming area with medieval buildings, narrow alleys, and significant historical landmarks dating back to Roman and medieval times.

Opening Hours
Open 24/7

Admission Fees
Free

Address & Location
Niederdorfstrasse, 8001 Zurich, Switzerland

Getting There
- By Tram: Lines 4, 15 to Rathaus
- By Bus: Bus 31 to Central

Why Visit
The Old Town offers a unique glimpse into Zurich's past with its well-preserved architecture, historic churches, and vibrant nightlife.

Outdoor Activities
- Walking tours
- Shopping
- Dining at local cafes

Pro Tips
- Join a guided walking tour to learn about the area's history.

- Going early in the morning is the best way to avoid crowds.

Don't Miss
- Grossmünster Church
- Fraumünster Church

Swiss National Museum (Landesmuseum)

The Swiss National Museum, established in 1898, showcases Switzerland's cultural history from ancient times to the present.

Opening Hours
- Tuesday-Sunday: 10:00 AM - 5:00 PM
- Thursday: 10:00 AM – 7:00 PM
- Closed on Monday

Admission Fees
- Adults: CHF 10
- Reduced: CHF 8
- Children under 16: Free

Address & Location
Museumstrasse 2, 8001 Zurich, Switzerland
Contact: +41 44 218 65 11

Getting There

- By Train: Zürich Hauptbahnhof (Main Station)
- By Tram: Lines 4, 6, 10 to HB

Why Visit

Tourists visit to explore exhibits ranging from prehistoric artifacts to contemporary art and learn about Swiss culture and history.

Outdoor Activities

Exploring the surrounding park

Pro Tips
- Check for special exhibitions and events.
- For those that want a more in-depth experience, there are audio tours available.

Don't Miss
- The Gothic and Baroque art collections
- The archaeology exhibit

Bahnhofstrasse

Bahnhofstrasse, established in 1864, is one of the world's most exclusive shopping streets, located in the heart of Zurich.

Opening Hours
- Monday-Friday: 9:00 AM – 8:00 PM

- Saturday: 9:00 AM – 6:00 PM
- Closed on Sunday

Admission Fees
Free

Address & Location
Bahnhofstrasse, 8001 Zurich, Switzerland

Getting There
- By Train: Zürich Hauptbahnhof
- By Tram: Lines 6, 7, 11, 13

Why Visit
Tourists visit Bahnhofstrasse for luxury shopping, dining, and people-watching in a vibrant urban setting.

Outdoor Activities
- Window shopping
- Dining at upscale restaurants

Pro Tips
- Visit during the Christmas season for beautiful decorations.
- Look out for street performances and events.

Don't Miss
- Paradeplatz, a major financial center

- Confiserie Sprüngli for exquisite chocolates

Uetliberg Mountain

Uetliberg has been a popular hiking destination since the 19th century, offering panoramic views of Zurich and the Alps.

Opening Hours
Open 24/7

Admission Fees
Free

Address & Location
Uetliberg, 8143 Zurich, Switzerland

Getting There
By Train: Sihltalbahn to Uetliberg station

Why Visit
Tourists visit Uetliberg for its breathtaking views, hiking trails, and outdoor activities.

Outdoor Activities
- Hiking
- Mountain biking
- Paragliding

Pro Tips
- Wear comfortable hiking shoes.
- Visit the Uetliberg lookout tower for the best views.

Don't Miss
- The Planet Trail, a walk through the solar system
- Views from the peak during sunrise or sunset

Kunsthaus Zurich

Kunsthaus Zurich, founded in 1910, houses one of the most important art collections in Switzerland, featuring works from the Middle Ages to contemporary art.

Opening Hours
- Tuesday, Friday to Sunday: 10:00 AM – 6:00 PM
- Wednesday to Thursday: 10:00 AM – 8:00 PM
- Closed on Monday

Admission Fees
- Adults: CHF 23

- Reduced: CHF 18
- Children under 16: Free

Address & Location
Heimplatz 1, 8001 Zurich, Switzerland
Contact: +41 44 253 84 84

Getting There
By Tram: Lines 3, 5, 9 to Kunsthaus

Why Visit
Art enthusiasts visit to see masterpieces by Swiss and international artists, including works by Giacometti, Monet, and Picasso.

Outdoor Activities
Explore the surrounding gardens

Pro Tips
- Check for temporary exhibitions and guided tours.
- Museum shops offer unique art-related souvenirs.

Don't Miss
- The Giacometti Hall
- The Chagall collection

Zurich Zoo

Zurich Zoo, established in 1929, is known for its naturalistic enclosures and diverse animal species from around the world.

Opening Hours
Daily: 9:00 AM – 6:00 PM

Admission Fees
- Adults: CHF 29
- Children (6-15): CHF 14
- Children under 6: Free

Address & Location
Zürichbergstrasse 221, 8044 Zurich, Switzerland
Contact: +41 44 254 25 00

Getting There
- By Tram: Line 6 to Zoo
- By Bus: Bus 751 to Zoo

Why Visit
Families and animal lovers visit Zurich Zoo for its engaging exhibits and conservation efforts.

Outdoor Activities
- Animal feeding sessions
- Guided tours

Pro Tips
- Arrive early to avoid the crowds.
- Wear comfortable walking shoes.

Don't Miss
- The Masoala Rainforest exhibit
- The elephant park

Fraumünster Church

Fraumünster Church, founded in 853 by King Louis the German, is famous for its stunning stained-glass windows by Marc Chagall.

Opening Hours
- Monday to Saturday: 10:00 AM – 5:00 PM
- Sunday: 12:00 PM – 5:00 PM

Admission Fees
- Adults: CHF 5
- Students: CHF 2
- Children under 16: Free

Address & Location
Münsterhof 2, 8001 Zurich, Switzerland
Contact: +41 44 211 41 00

Getting There
By Tram: Lines 4, 15 to Helmhaus

Why Visit
Tourists visit for its architectural beauty, historical significance, and the renowned Chagall windows.

Outdoor Activities
Exploring the adjacent Münsterhof square

Pro Tips
- Visit early in the day to enjoy the windows in natural light.
- Guided tours provide deeper insights into the church's history.

Don't Miss
- The Chagall windows
- The 13th-century frescoes

Lindenhof

Lindenhof has been a site of historical importance since Roman times, serving as a Roman fort and later as a medieval castle.

Opening Hours
Open 24/7

Admission Fees
Free

Address & Location
Lindenhof Hill, 8001 Zurich, Switzerland

Getting There
By Tram: Lines 6, 7, 10 to Central

Why Visit
Lindenhof offers panoramic views of Zurich's Old Town, the Limmat River, and the university quarter.

Outdoor Activities
- Relaxing in the park
- Chess playing on the outdoor boards

Pro Tips
- Enjoy a picnic in the park.
- Visit during sunset for beautiful views.

Don't Miss
- The view over the Old Town
- The Roman stone monument

Rietberg Museum

The Rietberg Museum, opened in 1952, is dedicated to non-European art and features collections from Asia, Africa, and Oceania.

Opening Hours
- Tuesday through Sunday: 10:00 AM – 5:00 PM
- Wednesday: 10:00 AM – 8:00 PM
- Closed on Monday

Admission Fees
- Adults: CHF 18
- Reduced: CHF 14
- Children under 16: Free

Address & Location
Gablerstrasse 15, 8002 Zurich, Switzerland
Contact: +41 44 415 31 31

Getting There
By Tram: Line 7 to Museum Rietberg

Why Visit
Art lovers and cultural enthusiasts visit for its unique collections and serene park setting.

Outdoor Activities
Strolling through the Rieterpark

Pro Tips
- Combine your visit with a walk through the adjacent park.
- Check for special exhibitions and events.

Don't Miss
- The Chinese and Japanese art collections
- The museum's villa architecture

Zurich offers a diverse array of attractions, from historical landmarks and world-class museums to stunning natural scenery and vibrant cultural hotspots. Whether you're interested in art, history, shopping, or outdoor activities, Zurich has something for every traveler. Plan your visit to these top attractions for an unforgettable experience in this beautiful Swiss city.

CHAPTER 5

Accommodation Options

Zurich is a city that caters to all types of travelers with a range of accommodations from luxurious hotels to budget-friendly hostels. Here's an overview of the different types of accommodations available in Zurich, followed by a detailed list of top recommendations in each category.

Luxury Hotels

Luxury hotels in Zurich offer world-class amenities, impeccable service, and prime locations, often with stunning views of the lake or city.

Baur au Lac
Price Range: CHF 700 - 1200 per night
Website: [Baur au Lac](https://www.bauraulac.ch/)
Address: Talstrasse 1, 8001 Zurich, Switzerland
Contact: +41 44 220 50 20
Description: This historic hotel offers luxurious rooms, a private park, and stunning views of Lake Zurich. Amenities include a gourmet restaurant, spa, and concierge service. Nearby attractions include the Bahnhofstrasse shopping street and the Opera House.

The Dolder Grand
Price Range: CHF 600 - 1100 per night
Website: [The Dolder Grand](https://www.thedoldergrand.com/)
Address: Kurhausstrasse 65, 8032 Zurich, Switzerland
Contact: +41 44 456 60 00
Description: Located in a picturesque hilltop setting, The Dolder Grand combines luxury with art. It offers a spa, fine dining, and panoramic views. Nearby attractions include the Zoo Zurich and the Kunsthaus Zurich.

Park Hyatt Zurich
Price Range: CHF 500 - 900 per night
Website: [Park Hyatt Zurich](https://www.hyatt.com/en-US/hotel/switzerland/park-hyatt-zurich/zurph)
Address: Beethovenstrasse 21, 8002 Zurich, Switzerland
Contact: +41 43 883 12 34
Description: This modern luxury hotel features spacious rooms, a wellness center, and an award-winning restaurant. It's located near the Bahnhofstrasse and Lake Zurich.

Savoy Baur en Ville
Price Range: CHF 400 - 800 per night

55

Website: [Savoy Baur en Ville](https://www.savoy-zuerich.ch/)
Address: Paradeplatz, 8001 Zurich, Switzerland
Contact: +41 44 215 25 25
Description: An elegant hotel with classic decor, located at the heart of Zurich. It offers a fine dining restaurant and a prime location close to the financial district and shopping areas.

Widder Hotel
Price Range: CHF 450 - 850 per night
Website: [Widder Hotel](https://www.widderhotel.com/)
Address: Rennweg 7, 8001 Zurich, Switzerland
Contact: +41 44 224 25 26
Description: A boutique hotel set in a cluster of historic buildings. It offers individually decorated rooms and suites, a gourmet restaurant, and a jazz bar. It's located in the Old Town, close to major attractions.

Mid-Range Hotels

Mid-range hotels provide comfort and convenience without breaking the bank. They typically offer good locations and essential amenities.

Hotel Glockenhof
Price Range: CHF 250 - 400 per night

Website: [Hotel Glockenhof](https://www.glockenhof.ch/)
Address: Sihlstrasse 31, 8001 Zurich, Switzerland
Contact: +41 44 225 91 91
Description: A contemporary hotel with modern amenities, including a garden, restaurant, and business facilities. It's located near the Bahnhofstrasse and Old Town.

Hotel Adler Zurich
Price Range: CHF 200 - 350 per night
Website: [Hotel Adler Zurich](https://www.hotel-adler.ch/)
Address: Rosengasse 10, 8001 Zurich, Switzerland
Contact: +41 44 266 96 96
Description: A charming hotel located in the heart of the Old Town, featuring individually decorated rooms and a cozy Swiss restaurant.

Hotel Montana Zurich
Price Range: CHF 150 - 300 per night
Website: [Hotel Montana Zurich](https://www.hotelmontana-zurich.com/)
Address: Konradstrasse 39, 8005 Zurich, Switzerland
Contact: +41 44 360 12 00
Description: A stylish hotel offering comfortable rooms and a convenient location near the main train station.

Hotel St. Josef
Price Range: CHF 180 - 320 per night
Website: [Hotel St. Josef](https://www.st-josef.ch/)
Address: Hirschengraben 64, 8001 Zurich, Switzerland
Contact: +41 44 250 57 57
Description: A cozy hotel with modern amenities, located close to the Old Town and University of Zurich.

Hotel City Zurich
Price Range: CHF 200 - 350 per night
Website: [Hotel City Zurich](https://www.hotelcityzurich.ch/)
Address: Löwenstrasse 34, 8001 Zurich, Switzerland
Contact: +41 44 217 17 17
Description: A centrally located hotel with comfortable rooms and a stylish bar. It's near the Bahnhofstrasse and main attractions.

Budget Accommodations

Budget accommodations are ideal for travelers looking to save money. They provide basic but comfortable stays, often with fewer amenities.

easyHotel Zurich
Price Range: CHF 100 - 200 per night
Website: [easyHotel Zurich](https://www.easyhotel.com/hotels/switzerland/zurich)
Address: Zwinglistrasse 14, 8004 Zurich, Switzerland
Contact: +41 44 241 00 55
Description: A budget-friendly hotel offering basic yet comfortable rooms. It's located in the lively District 4.

Hotel Marta
Price Range: CHF 110 - 220 per night
Website: [Hotel Marta](https://www.hotelmarta.ch/)
Address: Zähringerstrasse 36, 8001 Zurich, Switzerland
Contact: +41 44 269 95 95
Description: A budget hotel with modern decor, located close to the Old Town and ETH Zurich.

Hotel Arlette Beim Hauptbahnhof
Price Range: CHF 120 - 230 per night
Website: [Hotel Arlette Beim Hauptbahnhof](http://www.hotelarlette.ch/)
Address: Stampfenbachstrasse 26, 8001 Zurich, Switzerland
Contact: +41 44 252 00 33

Description: A family-run hotel offering cozy rooms and friendly service, located near the main train station.

ibis Zurich City West
Price Range: CHF 130 - 250 per night
Website: [ibis Zurich City West](https://all.accor.com/hotel/2942/index.en.shtml)
Address: Schiffbaustrasse 11, 8005 Zurich, Switzerland
Contact: +41 44 276 21 00
Description: A budget hotel with modern amenities, located in the trendy Zurich West district.

Meininger Hotel Zurich Greencity
Price Range: CHF 100 - 210 per night
Website: [Meininger Hotel Zurich Greencity](https://www.meininger-hotels.com/en/hotels/zurich/greencity/)
Address: Maneggstrasse 9, 8041 Zurich, Switzerland
Contact: +41 43 508 58 80
Description: A new hotel offering budget-friendly rooms with modern amenities, located in the sustainable Green City district.

Hostels and Guesthouses

Hostels and guesthouses offer affordable stays with opportunities for social interaction, ideal for solo travelers and young adventurers.

Zurich Youth Hostel
Price Range: CHF 40 - 80 per night
Website: [Zurich Youth Hostel](https://www.youthhostel.ch/en/hostels/zurich/)
Address: Mutschellenstrasse 114, 8038

Zurich, Switzerland
Contact: +41 43 399 78 00
Description: A well-equipped hostel with dormitories and private rooms, located near the lake and public transport.

Oldtown Hostel Otter
Price Range: CHF 50 - 100 per night
Website: [Oldtown Hostel Otter](https://www.oldtown-hostel.ch/)
Address: Oberdorfstrasse 7, 8001 Zurich, Switzerland
Contact: +41 44 251 22 07
Description: A centrally located hostel with a lively bar and comfortable dorms and private rooms.

Langstars Backpackers
Price Range: CHF 35 - 75 per night
Website: [Langstars Backpackers](http://www.langstars.ch/)
Address: Langstrasse 120, 8004 Zurich, Switzerland
Contact: +41 43 534 49 24
Description: A vibrant hostel located in the heart of Zurich's nightlife district, offering budget accommodation with a bar.

Green Marmot Capsule Hotel
Price Range: CHF 45 - 85 per night
Website: [Green Marmot Capsule Hotel](https://greenmarmot.com/)
Address: Schifflände 26, 8001 Zurich, Switzerland
Contact: +41 44 221 03 11
Description: A unique capsule hotel offering compact yet comfortable sleeping pods, located in the Old Town.

Budget Hostel Zurich
Price Range: CHF 40 - 80 per night
Website: [Budget Hostel Zurich](https://www.budgethostelzurich.ch/)
Address: Riedenhaldenstrasse 7, 8046 Zurich, Switzerland
Contact: +41 44 364 33 00

Description: A simple and affordable hostel offering basic amenities and a communal kitchen, located in a quiet neighborhood.

Unique Stays

Unique stays include boutique hotels, Airbnb properties, and vacation rentals. These offer a more personalized experience, often with unique decor and local charm.

25hours Hotel Langstrasse
Price Range: CHF 180 - 350 per night
Website: [25hours Hotel Langstrasse](https://www.25hours-hotels.com/en/hotels/zurich/langstrasse)
Address: Langstrasse 150, 8004 Zurich, Switzerland
Contact: +41 44 576 50 00
Description: A trendy boutique hotel with quirky decor, located in the lively Langstrasse area. It features a rooftop bar and restaurant.

Hotel Helvetia
Price Range: CHF 170 - 300 per night
Website: [Hotel Helvetia](https://www.hotel-helvetia.ch/)
Address: Stauffacherquai 1, 8004 Zurich, Switzerland
Contact: +41 44 297 99 98

Description: A stylish boutique hotel with individually designed rooms and a popular restaurant, located near the Sihl River.

Atlantis by Giardino
Price Range: CHF 250 - 450 per night
Website: [Atlantis by Giardino](https://www.atlantisbygiardino.ch/)
Address: Döltschiweg 234, 8055 Zurich, Switzerland
Contact: +41 44 456 55 55
Description: A luxury boutique hotel with modern amenities, located at the foot of the Uetliberg Mountain. It offers a spa, outdoor pool, and gourmet dining.

Hotel Plattenhof
Price Range: CHF 150 - 280 per night
Website: [Hotel Plattenhof](https://www.plattenhof.ch/)
Address: Plattenstrasse 26, 8032 Zurich, Switzerland
Contact: +41 44 251 19 10
Description: A cozy boutique hotel with contemporary design, located near the University of Zurich and the ETH.

Airbnb Zurich City Loft
Price Range: CHF 100 - 300 per night

Website: [Airbnb](https://www.airbnb.com)
Address: Available upon booking
Description: Modern lofts and apartments located throughout the city, offering a home-like experience with kitchen facilities and personalized decor.

Neighborhood Guide

Old Town (Altstadt): Best for historical charm and central location.
Enge: Family-friendly area with parks and proximity to Lake Zurich.
District 4 (Langstrasse): Vibrant nightlife and diverse dining options.
Seefeld: Upscale area with easy access to the lake and cultural attractions.

Best Areas to Stay
Old Town (Altstadt)
Description: The historical heart of Zurich with cobblestone streets, medieval buildings, and major landmarks. Ideal for first-time visitors.
Nearby Attractions: Grossmünster, Fraumünster, Bahnhofstrasse

Enge
Description: A family-friendly neighborhood with parks, museums, and proximity to Lake Zurich.

Nearby Attractions: Rietberg Museum, Belvoir Park, Arboretum

District 4 (Langstrasse)
Description: Known for its vibrant nightlife, diverse dining options, and artistic vibe. Suitable for younger travelers.
Nearby Attractions: Langstrasse nightlife, Kanzlei Flea Market, Museum of Design

Seefeld
Description: An upscale area with lakeside promenades, cultural attractions, and gourmet restaurants. Ideal for a more relaxed stay.
Nearby Attractions: Zurich Opera House, Chinese Garden, Seefeldquai

Family-Friendly Locations
Enge
Description: Offers parks, playgrounds, and family-friendly attractions like the Rietberg Museum and Lake Zurich.
Nearby Accommodations: Park Hyatt Zurich, Hotel Ascot

Seefeld
Description: Quiet and safe, with easy access to outdoor activities and cultural sites.

Nearby Accommodations: Eden au Lac, Hotel Seegarten

Zurich West

Description: Modern and trendy, with family-friendly attractions like Technorama and Schiffbau.

Nearby Accommodations: Novotel Zurich City-West, Sheraton Zurich Hotel

In Zurich, whether you are seeking luxury, mid-range, budget, or unique stays, there's a wide array of options to suit every traveler's needs and preferences. Enjoy your stay in this stunning Swiss city!

CHAPTER 6

Hidden Gems and Local Favorites

Zurich is a city known for its pristine lakes, stunning architecture, and bustling financial district. However, beyond the well-trodden paths of Bahnhofstrasse and the Old Town, there are numerous hidden gems and local favorites that offer a more authentic and unique experience of the city. Here's a guide to Zurich's off-the-beaten-path neighborhoods, unique cafes, and restaurants that travelers need to know about.

Off-the-Beaten-Path Neighborhoods

Kreis 4 (Langstrasse Quarter)

Kreis 4 is known for its vibrant and diverse atmosphere. Once considered Zurich's red-light district, it has transformed into a lively area full of eclectic bars, restaurants, and shops. It's perfect for those looking to experience Zurich's nightlife and cultural diversity.

Highlights: Street art, international cuisine, live music venues, and the bustling Langstrasse.
Must-Visit Spots: Kanzlei Flea Market, Hive Club, and the Museum of Design.

68

Wipkingen

Wipkingen is a charming residential neighborhood located along the Limmat River. It offers a peaceful retreat with plenty of green spaces and a community vibe.

Highlights: Riverside parks, local markets, and scenic views.
Must-Visit Spots: Wipkingerpark, Nordbrücke café, and the Freitag Tower.

Höngg

Höngg is a hilly neighborhood with a village-like feel. It's known for its vineyards, orchards, and beautiful views over Zurich.

Highlights: Walking trails, local wineries, and historical sites.
Must-Visit Spots: Hönggerberg, Hohenklingen Castle, and the Stadtgärtnerei (City Nursery).

Albisrieden

Albisrieden offers a blend of old-world charm and modern living. It's a lesser-known area that's perfect for those looking to explore Zurich's quieter side.

Highlights: Traditional Swiss houses, local eateries, and tranquil parks.

Must-Visit Spots: Albisrieden Church, Uetliberg hiking trails, and the local weekly market.

Wollishofen

Wollishofen, located on the western shores of Lake Zurich, is known for its artsy vibe and lakeside charm. It's home to artists, musicians, and creative professionals.

Highlights: Art studios, lakeside promenades, and cultural festivals.

Must-Visit Spots: Rote Fabrik cultural center, Strandbad Mythenquai (beach), and the BrunauPark.

Unique Cafes

Café Lang

Address: Limmatplatz 7, 8005 Zurich

Description: Café Lang is a trendy spot in Kreis 5, known for its stylish interior, excellent coffee, and delicious pastries. It's a great place to relax and people-watch.

Must-Try: Cappuccino and homemade croissants.

Babu's Bakery & Coffeehouse

Address: Löwenstrasse 1, 8001 Zurich

Description: A popular spot for breakfast and brunch, Babu's offers a cozy atmosphere with a

vintage touch. Their homemade bread and cakes are a hit among locals.
Must-Try: Avocado toast and carrot cake.

Café des Amis
Address: Nordstrasse 88, 8037 Zurich
Description: Located in Wipkingen, this café is a local favorite for its relaxed ambiance and excellent brunch options. The outdoor seating area is perfect in summer.
Must-Try: Eggs Benedict and freshly squeezed orange juice.

Sphères
Address: Hardturmstrasse 66, 8005 Zurich
Description: Sphères is a unique blend of a café, bar, and bookstore. It's a creative space where you can enjoy a cup of coffee while browsing through books and magazines.
Must-Try: Their signature hot chocolate and homemade quiches.

Milchbar
Address: Kappelergasse 16, 8001 Zurich
Description: Tucked away in the Old Town, Milchbar is known for its artisanal coffee and tranquil courtyard. It's an ideal spot for a quiet coffee break.
Must-Try: Flat white and the daily fresh pastries.

Unique Restaurants

Restaurant Volkshaus
Address: Stauffacherstrasse 60, 8004 Zurich
Description: Housed in a historic building, Volkshaus offers a mix of traditional Swiss and modern European cuisine. It's known for its elegant interior and lively atmosphere.
Must-Try: Züri-Geschnetzeltes (sliced veal with creamy mushroom sauce) and their extensive wine list.

Hiltl
Address: Sihlstrasse 28, 8001 Zurich
Description: Hiltl is the world's oldest vegetarian restaurant, offering a diverse menu of vegetarian and vegan dishes. It's a must-visit for health-conscious foodies.
Must-Try: Hiltl's famous vegetarian buffet and freshly pressed juices.

Frau Gerolds Garten
Address: Geroldstrasse 23, 8005 Zurich
Description: An urban garden and restaurant, Frau Gerolds Garten is a unique dining spot with outdoor seating, local craft beers, and seasonal dishes.
Must-Try: Grilled specialties and local craft beers.

Maison Manesse
Address: Hopfenstrasse 2, 8045 Zurich
Description: A Michelin-starred restaurant known for its creative and modern cuisine. Maison Manesse offers a unique dining experience with a focus on seasonal ingredients.
Must-Try: Tasting menu with wine pairing.

Rosso
Address: Geroldstrasse 31, 8005 Zurich
Description: Located in an industrial setting, Rosso is famous for its wood-fired pizzas and laid-back atmosphere. It's a popular spot among locals for casual dining.
Must-Try: Truffle pizza and their homemade tiramisu.

Exploring Zurich's hidden gems and local favorites provides a deeper and more authentic experience of the city. From off-the-beaten-path neighborhoods to unique cafes and restaurants, these lesser-known spots offer a glimpse into the local culture and lifestyle. Whether you're a first-time visitor or a seasoned traveler, make sure to add these recommendations to your Zurich itinerary for a truly memorable trip.

CHAPTER 7

Cultural Experiences

Zurich is a city rich in cultural heritage, offering a vibrant mix of museums, galleries, performing arts venues, and local festivals. Immerse yourself in the city's dynamic cultural scene with these must-visit attractions and events.

Museums and Galleries

Kunsthaus Zurich

Description: One of Switzerland's most important art museums, Kunsthaus Zurich houses an extensive collection of European art from the Middle Ages to the present day. Highlights include works by Swiss artists like Alberto Giacometti and Ferdinand Hodler, as well as international masters such as Picasso, Monet, and Van Gogh.
Address: Heimplatz 1, 8001 Zurich

Swiss National Museum (Landesmuseum)

Description: Explore Switzerland's cultural history at the Swiss National Museum, housed in a stunning neo-Gothic building. The museum's exhibits cover a wide range of topics, including Swiss art, history, and culture, with artifacts dating back to prehistoric times.

Address: Museumstrasse 2, 8001 Zurich

Museum Rietberg
Description: Located in a historic villa surrounded by a scenic park, Museum Rietberg is dedicated to non-European art and culture. Its diverse collection includes artifacts from Asia, Africa, the Americas, and Oceania, offering visitors a unique perspective on global art and heritage.
Address: Gablerstrasse 15, 8002 Zurich

Helmhaus Zurich
Description: A contemporary art gallery situated in a historic building overlooking Lake Zurich, Helmhaus Zurich showcases innovative works by local and international artists. The gallery hosts regular exhibitions, focusing on various themes and artistic movements.
Address: Limmatquai 31, 8001 Zurich

Haus Konstruktiv
Description: Dedicated to concrete, constructive, and conceptual art, Haus Konstruktiv presents cutting-edge contemporary artworks in a renovated industrial building. The museum's exhibitions explore the intersection of art, architecture, and design, providing insight into modern artistic practices.
Address: Selnaustrasse 25, 8001 Zurich

Performing Arts

Opernhaus Zurich (Zurich Opera House)
Description: Renowned for its world-class productions and stunning architecture, the Zurich Opera House is a cultural landmark in the heart of the city. It hosts a diverse program of opera, ballet, and classical music performances throughout the year.
Address: Falkenstrasse 1, 8008 Zurich

Schauspielhaus Zürich (Zürich Playhouse)
Description: Switzerland's largest theater, Schauspielhaus Zurich is known for its innovative and thought-provoking productions. From classic plays to contemporary works, the theater offers a diverse repertoire that appeals to theater enthusiasts of all ages.
Address: Pfauenstrasse 12, 8001 Zürich

Tonhalle-Orchester Zürich (Tonhalle Orchestra Zurich)
Description: Experience the magic of classical music at the Tonhalle Zurich, home to one of Europe's leading orchestras. The venue's acoustically renowned concert hall hosts

performances by internationally acclaimed musicians and conductors.
Address: Claridenstrasse 7, 8002 Zurich

Kaufleuten
Description: A cultural hotspot in Zurich, Kaufleuten is a historic venue that hosts a variety of events, including live music concerts, DJ nights, theater performances, and art exhibitions. It's a favorite destination for both locals and visitors seeking entertainment and cultural experiences.
Address: Pelikanstrasse 18, 8001 Zurich

Moods Jazz Club
Description: For jazz enthusiasts, Moods Jazz Club is the place to be in Zurich. Situated in the Schiffbau cultural complex, the club offers intimate concerts featuring top international jazz artists, as well as up-and-coming talents from the local scene.
Address: Schiffbaustrasse 6, 8005 Zurich

Local Festivals

Street Parade
Description: One of Europe's largest techno music festivals, the Street Parade is a colorful celebration of electronic dance music, love, and unity. Every August, thousands of revelers gather in Zurich to

dance through the streets to the beats of world-renowned DJs and live performers.
Location: Parade route through the city center

Zurich Film Festival
Description: A highlight on Zurich's cultural calendar, the Zurich Film Festival showcases a diverse selection of international and Swiss films, including premieres, retrospectives, and documentary features. The festival also hosts Q&A sessions, industry panels, and networking events for film enthusiasts and industry professionals.
Location: Various venues across Zurich

Sechseläuten
Description: Held annually in April, Sechseläuten is a traditional spring festival that marks the end of winter and the beginning of the warmer months. The highlight of the event is the Sechseläutenzug, a colorful parade featuring guilds, horse-drawn carriages, and historical costumes. The festival culminates in the burning of the Böögg, a symbolic figure representing winter.
Location: Sechseläutenplatz, Zurich

Zurich Festival (Zürcher Festspiele)
Description: A multi-disciplinary arts festival, the Zurich Festival showcases a diverse program of music, theater, dance, and visual arts. From classical

concerts to avant-garde performances, the festival offers something for everyone, attracting both local and international artists and audiences.

Location: Various venues across Zurich

Knabenschiessen
Description: Dating back to the 17th century, Knabenschiessen is a traditional marksmanship competition held annually in September. The event brings together sharpshooters from across Switzerland to compete for the title of Knabenschiessen King or Queen. In addition to the shooting competition, the festival features carnival rides, food stalls, and entertainment for the whole family.

Location: Albisgüetli Shooting Range, Zurich

Zurich's cultural scene is as diverse as it is dynamic, offering a wealth of museums, galleries, performing arts venues, and local festivals for visitors to explore and enjoy. Whether you're a fan of classical art or contemporary music, there's something for everyone in this vibrant Swiss city. Don't miss out on these cultural experiences during your stay in Zurich!

CHAPTER 8

Outdoor Activities

Zurich, with its stunning natural landscapes and well-maintained recreational facilities, is a paradise for outdoor enthusiasts. Whether you're into hiking, biking, water sports, or winter activities, the city offers a variety of options to suit all tastes and skill levels. Here's a guide to some of the best outdoor activities you can enjoy in and around Zurich.

Hiking and Walking Trails

Uetliberg Mountain

Description: Uetliberg, Zurich's local mountain, offers breathtaking views of the city and Lake Zurich. It's a popular spot for hiking and walking.

Trail Highlights:
- Planet Trail: A 6-kilometer trail depicting the solar system, leading from Uetliberg to Felsenegg.
- Uetliberg to Triemli: A 2-hour walk down the mountain, offering beautiful forest scenery.

How to Get There: Take the S10 train from Zurich HB to Uetliberg station.

Sihlwald Nature Park

Description: A serene forest area perfect for leisurely walks and hikes. It features well-marked trails and a visitor center.

Trail Highlights:
- Langenberg Wildpark: A wildlife park with free-roaming native animals.
- Panorama Trail: Offers stunning views of the Sihl Valley.

How to Get There: Take the S4 train from Zurich HB to Sihlwald station.

Biking Routes

Lake Zurich Loop

Description: A scenic 66-kilometer loop around Lake Zurich, suitable for cyclists of all levels. It offers picturesque views of the lake and the surrounding mountains.

Route Highlights:
- Seebad Utoquai: A popular lakeside bathing area.
- Rapperswil: A charming town known for its medieval castle and rose gardens.

How to Get There: Start from Zurich and follow the well-marked cycling paths around the lake.

Zurich to Rhine Falls

Description: A longer route (about 70 kilometers) that takes you from Zurich to Europe's largest waterfall, the Rhine Falls.

Route Highlights:
- Winterthur: A city with a rich cultural scene and beautiful parks.
- Rhine Falls: Stunning natural spectacle and boat trips.

How to Get There: Start from Zurich and follow the designated cycling paths towards Schaffhausen.

Water Sports on Lake Zurich

Swimming and Sunbathing
Locations:
Seebad Enge: Offers a beach area, floating platforms, and a sauna.
Tiefenbrunnen: Features a family-friendly swimming area and a restaurant.

Activities: Swimming, sunbathing, and enjoying the facilities.

Stand-Up Paddleboarding (SUP)
Locations:
SUP Station Zurich: Offers rentals and lessons.
SUP Center Zollikon: Another great rental spot with calm waters.

Activities: Paddleboarding on the lake, exploring the shoreline.

Sailing and Boating
Locations:
Lake Zurich Sailing School: Offers sailing courses and boat rentals.
Pedalo Rentals: Available at various points along the lake, including Bürkliplatz.

Activities: Sailing, renting pedalos, and motorboats.

Winter Sports
Skiing and Snowboarding Nearby

Flumserberg
Description: A popular ski resort offering a variety of slopes for all skill levels.

Facilities: Ski and snowboard rentals, ski schools, and après-ski options.

How to Get There: About 90 minutes by train from Zurich to Unterterzen, then take the gondola up to the resort.

Engelberg-Titlis

Description: Known for its excellent snow conditions and diverse terrain.

Facilities: Ski rentals, snow parks, and a variety of dining options.

How to Get There: About 2 hours by train from Zurich to Engelberg.

Ice Skating Rinks

Dolder Sports

Description: A large outdoor ice rink located at the Dolder Grand Hotel.

Facilities: Skate rentals, curling, and a cozy restaurant.

How to Get There: Take the Dolderbahn from Römerhof to the Dolder Grand.

Heuried Ice Rink

Description: A modern ice skating facility with both indoor and outdoor rinks.

Facilities: Skate rentals and a café.

How to Get There: Accessible by tram (Line 9) or bus (Line 32).

Parks and Gardens

Zurich Botanical Garden

Description: A tranquil oasis featuring over 15,000 species of plants from around the world. It includes greenhouses, themed gardens, and a pond.

Activities: Guided tours, educational exhibits, and peaceful walks.

How to Get There: Take tram line 2 or 4 to Höschgasse, then a short walk.

Chinese Garden

Description: A beautiful garden gifted by Zurich's Chinese sister city, Kunming. It features traditional Chinese architecture, a pond, and a pavilion.

Activities: Strolls, photography, and relaxation.

How to Get There: Take tram line 2 or 4 to Fröhlichstrasse, then a short walk.

Zurich offers a wealth of outdoor activities that cater to nature lovers, adventure seekers, and those looking to relax in beautiful surroundings. Whether you're hiking up mountains, cycling around lakes, enjoying water sports, or exploring botanical gardens, Zurich provides endless opportunities for outdoor fun. Make sure to include some of these activities in your itinerary to experience the best of Zurich's natural beauty.

CHAPTER 9

Day Trips and Excursions

Zurich's central location makes it an ideal base for exploring some of Switzerland's most picturesque and culturally rich destinations. Here are some must-visit day trips and excursions from Zurich that will add depth and variety to your Swiss adventure.

Lucerne

Lucerne, nestled between a beautiful lake and towering mountains, is one of Switzerland's most charming cities. Known for its preserved medieval architecture, stunning views, and vibrant cultural scene, Lucerne offers a perfect blend of nature and history.

Highlights
Chapel Bridge (Kapellbrücke): A picturesque wooden bridge dating back to the 14th century, adorned with historic paintings.
Old Town: Explore cobblestone streets, colorful buildings, and medieval towers.
Lake Lucerne: Enjoy a boat cruise or a stroll along the lakeside promenade.

Lion Monument: A poignant sculpture commemorating Swiss Guards who died during the French Revolution.

Getting There

By Train: Approximately 50 minutes from Zurich's main station (Zürich HB).
By Car: Around 45 minutes via A4.

Pro Tips

Don't Miss: The Swiss Transport Museum, offering an extensive collection of exhibits on all forms of transport.
Activities: Take a cable car ride up to Mount Pilatus or Mount Rigi for panoramic views.

Rhine Falls

The Rhine Falls, Europe's largest waterfall, is a spectacular natural attraction located near the town of Schaffhausen. The thunderous power and breathtaking beauty of the falls make it a must-see destination.

Highlights

Boat Trips: Get up close to the falls on a thrilling boat ride.
Viewing Platforms: Enjoy various perspectives from platforms on both sides of the falls.

Schloss Laufen: Visit the castle for more viewpoints and historical exhibits.

Getting There
By Train: Approximately 1 hour from Zurich to Schloss Laufen am Rheinfall station.
By Car: Around 45 minutes via A4.

Pro Tips
Don't Miss: The illuminated falls at night during summer months.
Activities: Hike the trails surrounding the falls for different vantage points.

Mount Titlis

Mount Titlis, known for its eternal snow and stunning glacier views, offers an unforgettable alpine experience. The mountain features a range of activities suitable for all seasons.

Highlights
Titlis Rotair: The world's first revolving cable car, providing 360-degree views.
Glacier Cave: Walk through a fascinating ice tunnel inside the glacier.
Cliff Walk: Europe's highest suspension bridge offers thrilling views.

Getting There

By Train: Approximately 2 hours from Zurich to Engelberg, then take the cable car.
By Car: Around 1.5 hours via A2.

Pro Tips

Don't Miss: The Ice Flyer chairlift for a close look at the glacier.
Activities: Skiing in winter, hiking, and mountain biking in summer.

Rapperswil-Jona

Rapperswil-Jona, often called the "town of roses," is located on the upper end of Lake Zurich. This picturesque town is known for its medieval castle, beautiful rose gardens, and lakeside charm.

Highlights

Rapperswil Castle: Explore the historic castle and enjoy panoramic views of Lake Zurich.
Rose Gardens: Over 15,000 rose bushes in various gardens throughout the town.
Lake Promenade: Stroll along the scenic lakeside and enjoy the tranquil atmosphere.

Getting There

By Train: Approximately 40 minutes from Zurich's main station (Zürich HB).

By Boat: Enjoy a leisurely boat ride from Zurich, taking about 2 hours.

Pro Tips

Don't Miss: The wooden bridge connecting Rapperswil to Hurden for a scenic walk.
Activities: Visit the Knie's Children's Zoo for a family-friendly outing.

Appenzell and Ebenalp

Appenzell, a picturesque village known for its well-preserved traditions and stunning landscapes, offers a quintessential Swiss experience. Ebenalp, the highest peak in the Appenzell Alps, provides breathtaking views and unique hiking opportunities.

Highlights

Appenzell Village: Explore the colorful houses, local shops, and traditional cheese dairies.
Ebenalp: Hike to the Wildkirchli caves and the famous Aescher cliff restaurant.
Santis Mountain: Accessible via cable car, offering panoramic views of six countries.

Getting There

By Train: Approximately 2 hours from Zurich to Appenzell, then take the cable car to Ebenalp.
By Car: Around 1.5 hours via A1 and A13.

Pro Tips

Don't Miss: Try the local Appenzeller cheese and visit the Appenzell Museum.

Activities: Hiking, paragliding, and exploring traditional crafts.

Winterthur

Winterthur, Switzerland's sixth-largest city, is known for its rich industrial heritage, vibrant cultural scene, and numerous museums. It's an ideal destination for art and history enthusiasts.

Highlights

Technorama: An interactive science and technology museum, great for families.

Fotomuseum Winterthur: One of the leading photography museums in Europe.

Old Town: Wander through the charming pedestrian zone with shops, cafes, and historical buildings.

Getting There

By Train: Approximately 20 minutes from Zurich's main station (Zürich HB).

By Car: Around 30 minutes via A1.

Pro Tips

Don't Miss: The Oskar Reinhart Collection, featuring an impressive collection of European art.
Activities: Visit the beautiful Stadtpark for a relaxing break.

Zurich's proximity to numerous fascinating destinations makes it an ideal hub for day trips and excursions. Whether you're drawn to charming medieval towns, stunning natural wonders, or vibrant cultural centers, the areas surrounding Zurich offer a wealth of experiences that cater to all interests. Make sure to plan your trips and enjoy the diversity and beauty of Switzerland beyond Zurich.

CHAPTER 10

Shopping

Zurich is a shopper's paradise, offering a diverse range of retail experiences that cater to all tastes and budgets. From luxury boutiques on one of the world's most exclusive shopping streets to charming independent shops showcasing local designers, Zurich's shopping scene is both vibrant and varied. Whether you're hunting for high-end fashion, unique souvenirs, or delicious Swiss chocolate, this guide will help you navigate Zurich's best shopping districts and hidden gems.

Popular Shopping Districts

Bahnhofstrasse
Location: Stretching from Zurich Hauptbahnhof (Main Station) to Lake Zurich.

Bahnhofstrasse is Zurich's most famous shopping street and one of the world's most exclusive retail avenues. This mile-long boulevard is lined with luxury boutiques, high-end department stores, and international flagship stores.

What to Look For:
Luxury Fashion: Brands like Chanel, Gucci, Prada, and Louis Vuitton.
Swiss Watches: Boutiques such as Bucherer and Beyer Chronometrie.
Department Stores: Globus and Jelmoli offer a wide range of luxury goods.

Niederdorf and Old Town (Altstadt)
Location: East of Bahnhofstrasse, in Zurich's historic district.

Niederdorf and the surrounding Old Town area offer a more eclectic shopping experience, with narrow, cobblestone streets filled with independent boutiques, artisan shops, and local designers.

What to Look For:
Independent Boutiques: Unique fashion and accessories from local designers.
Artisan Shops: Handcrafted goods, jewelry, and bespoke items.
Souvenirs: Traditional Swiss gifts, from cuckoo clocks to hand-painted cowbells.

Zurich West
Location: The western part of the city, near the Hardbrücke train station.

Once an industrial area, Zurich West has transformed into a trendy neighborhood known for its avant-garde boutiques, design shops, and vibrant nightlife.

What to Look For:
Concept Stores: Im Viadukt, a series of shops set within a repurposed railway viaduct.
Design Shops: Contemporary furniture and home decor from local designers.
Fashion Boutiques: Cutting-edge fashion and accessories.

Independent Boutiques and Local Designers

For those seeking unique and locally crafted items, Zurich's independent boutiques and local designers offer an array of distinctive products. These shops are scattered throughout the city, particularly in Niederdorf and Zurich West.

Top Boutiques:
Freitag: Known for its trendy bags made from recycled truck tarps.
Steinmauer: A boutique offering clothing and accessories from emerging Swiss designers.
Sibler: A treasure trove of Swiss-designed kitchenware and home accessories.

Souvenirs and Swiss Specialties

No trip to Zurich is complete without picking up some quintessentially Swiss souvenirs. From world-renowned Swiss watches to delicious chocolate, these specialties make perfect gifts and mementos.

Top Picks:
Swiss Watches: Rolex, Patek Philippe, and Swatch for every budget.
Swiss Chocolate: Confiserie Sprüngli, Läderach, and Teuscher.
Swiss Army Knives: Victorinox stores offer a wide range of these iconic tools.

Shopping Malls and Department Stores

Zurich's shopping malls and department stores provide a convenient and comprehensive shopping experience, featuring a mix of international brands and local products.

Major Shopping Malls
Sihlcity: Located in Zurich South, offers over 80 stores, a cinema, and a wellness center.
Glattzentrum: Situated just outside Zurich in Wallisellen, one of the largest malls in Switzerland.

Department Stores

Globus: A high-end department store on Bahnhofstrasse with a wide range of luxury goods.
Jelmoli: Another upscale option, known for its gourmet food section and designer fashion.

Flea Markets and Vintage Shops

For a more eclectic and budget-friendly shopping experience, Zurich's flea markets and vintage shops are perfect. These venues offer everything from antique treasures to retro fashion.

Top Spots
Bürkliplatz Flea Market: Held on Saturdays from May to October, offering antiques, vintage items, and collectibles.
Kreislauf 4+5: An annual market in Zurich West, showcasing second-hand fashion, books, and furniture.
Vintage Shops: Stores like Mosi's Secondhand Boutique and Fizzen for unique vintage clothing and accessories.

Zurich's diverse shopping scene ensures that every visitor can find something special, whether it's a luxury watch on Bahnhofstrasse, a bespoke piece from a local designer, or a delicious box of Swiss chocolates. With its blend of high-end and eclectic shopping districts, Zurich promises an unforgettable retail experience. Enjoy your shopping adventures in this vibrant Swiss metropolis, and don't forget to explore beyond the main streets to discover hidden gems and local favorites. Happy shopping!

CHAPTER 11

Practical Information

Traveling to Zurich, Switzerland's largest city, is an exciting experience filled with stunning sights, rich history, and vibrant culture. To help you navigate your visit smoothly, here's a comprehensive guide covering essential practical information.

Language Tips

Official Languages
German: The main language spoken in Zurich.
English: Widely understood and spoken, especially in tourist areas.
French and Italian: Also official languages in Switzerland, but less common in Zurich.

Key Phrases
Hello: Hallo
Goodbye: Auf Wiedersehen
Please: Bitte
Thank you: Danke
Yes: Ja
No: Nein
Do you speak English?: Sprechen Sie Englisch?
How much does this cost?: Wie viel kostet das?

Emergency Contacts

Important Numbers
Police: 117
Fire Department: 118
Ambulance: 144
European Emergency Number: 112 (works for all types of emergencies)
Pharmacy on Duty: 0848 134 134

Local Etiquette and Customs

Social Norms
Punctuality: Highly valued; always be on time.
Quietness: Keep noise levels low in public places, especially on public transport.
Greetings: A firm handshake with eye contact is common. Friends may greet with three kisses on the cheek.
Respect for Privacy: Swiss people value their privacy and personal space.

Dining Etiquette
Table Manners: Wait for everyone to be served before starting to eat. It's polite to say "Guten Appetit" before eating.
Paying the Bill: Usually, the host pays. Splitting the bill is less common but becoming more accepted among younger people.

Electricity and Plug Types

Specifications
Voltage: 230V
Frequency: 50Hz
Plug Types: Type C (two-pin) and Type J (three-pin). Adapters may be necessary for travelers from countries with different plug types.

Health and Safety

General Safety
Zurich is considered very safe, with low crime rates. Use common sense: keep an eye on belongings, especially in crowded areas.

Health Care
Pharmacies: Widely available, with many open 24/7.
Hospitals: Excellent medical facilities. Emergency care is easily accessible.

Vaccinations
No special vaccinations are required for travelers from most countries. However, routine vaccinations (MMR, diphtheria-tetanus-pertussis, varicella, polio, annual flu shot) are recommended.

Internet and SIM Cards

Internet Access
Free Wi-Fi is available in many public places, including cafes, restaurants, and hotels.
Public Wi-Fi: Available at the Zurich main train station (Zürich HB) and other locations.

SIM Cards
Major providers: Swisscom, Sunrise, Salt.
SIM cards can be purchased at airports, major train stations, and mobile phone shops.

Accessibility Information

Public Transport
Zurich's public transport system (ZVV) is highly accessible, with ramps, lifts, and designated spaces for wheelchair users.
SBB Assistance: Provides help for travelers with disabilities at major train stations.

Attractions
Many museums, hotels, and public buildings are equipped for accessibility. Always check ahead to ensure specific needs are met.

Currency
Swiss Franc (CHF)
Symbol: CHF

Subdivision: 100 centimes

Public Holidays

Major Public Holidays
New Year's Day: January 1
Good Friday: Variable
Easter Monday: Variable
Labor Day: May 1
Ascension Day: 40 days after Easter
Whit Monday: 50 days after Easter
Swiss National Day: August 1
Christmas Day: December 25
St. Stephen's Day: December 26

Money Matters

ATMs
Widely available throughout the city.
Most ATMs accept international cards (Visa, MasterCard).

Changing Money
Currency exchange services are available at banks, airports, train stations, and major hotels.
Exchange rates and fees vary, so compare options.

Credit Cards
Accepted widely in hotels, restaurants, and shops.

Visa and MasterCard are most common, followed by American Express.

Tipping

Not obligatory, but appreciated.
Restaurants: Service is included in the bill, but rounding up to the nearest franc or adding 5-10% is common for good service.
Taxis: Rounding up to the nearest franc.
Hotels: A small tip for exceptional service is appreciated.

Dos and Don'ts

Dos

Do use public transportation: Efficient, clean, and reliable.
Do greet with a handshake: When meeting someone for the first time.
Do carry cash: Especially for small purchases.
Do try local food: Enjoy Swiss specialties like cheese fondue and chocolate.
Do recycle: Use the recycling bins provided for different types of waste.

Don'ts

Don't be late: Punctuality is important.
Don't speak loudly: Maintain a quiet demeanor in public places.

Don't litter: Zurich is known for its cleanliness.
Don't jaywalk: Always use pedestrian crossings.

With this practical information, you're well-prepared for a smooth and enjoyable visit to Zurich. Whether navigating language barriers, adhering to local customs, or managing money matters, these tips will help you make the most of your time in this beautiful Swiss city. Enjoy your trip!

7-Day Itinerary for Zurich

Zurich, Switzerland's largest city, is an enchanting blend of historical charm and modern sophistication. Nestled on the shores of Lake Zurich and set against the backdrop of the Swiss Alps, Zurich offers a rich tapestry of cultural experiences, outdoor adventures, and culinary delights. Whether you're a history buff, an art enthusiast, or a nature lover, Zurich has something for everyone. This seven-day itinerary is designed to help you make the most of your visit, with detailed daily plans, cost estimates, and dining recommendations.

Day 1: Arrival and Exploring Old Town (Altstadt)
Cost of Spending:
Transportation: CHF 10 (public transport day pass)
Attractions: CHF 20 (entrance fees)
Meals: CHF 50
Total: CHF 80

Getting There:
From Zurich Airport, take the S-Bahn (S2, S16) to Zurich Hauptbahnhof (Zurich HB). Purchase a Zurich Card for unlimited public transport and discounted entry to various attractions.

What to Know:
Bahnhofstrasse: One of the world's most exclusive shopping streets.
Lindenhof: A historical site with panoramic views of the city.
Fraumünster Church: Famous for its Chagall stained-glass windows.
Grossmünster Church: An iconic twin-towered landmark.

Where to Eat:
Lunch: Sprüngli on Bahnhofstrasse for traditional Swiss pastries.
Dinner: Zeughauskeller, offering hearty Swiss cuisine in a historic armory.

Day 2: Art and Culture
Cost of Spending:
Transportation: CHF 10
Attractions: CHF 30
Meals: CHF 60
Total: CHF 100

Getting There:
Use your Zurich Card to access public transport.

What to Know:

Kunsthaus Zurich: Home to one of Switzerland's most important art collections.
Swiss National Museum: Offers insights into Swiss cultural history.
Cabaret Voltaire: The birthplace of the Dada art movement.

Where to Eat:
Lunch: Kronenhalle, renowned for its art-adorned walls and classic Swiss dishes.
Dinner: Raclette Factory for a traditional Swiss raclette experience.

Day 3: Day Trip to Lucerne
Cost of Spending:
Transportation: CHF 50 (round-trip train fare)
Attractions: CHF 20
Meals: CHF 60
Total: CHF 130

Getting There:
Take a train from Zurich HB to Lucerne (approx. 50 minutes).

What to Know:
Chapel Bridge (Kapellbrücke): A picturesque wooden bridge.
Lion Monument: A Swiss Guards memorial sculpture, with its poignant and tearful spirit.

Old Town: Explore the colorful medieval architecture.

Where to Eat:
Lunch: Wirtshaus Galliker, serving traditional Lucerne cuisine.
Dinner: Zunfthausrestaurant Pfistern, offering regional specialties with a view of the Reuss River.

Day 4: Hiking Uetliberg
Cost of Spending:
Transportation: CHF 20 (round-trip S-Bahn ticket)
Meals: CHF 50
Total: CHF 70

Getting There:
Take the S10 train from Zurich HB to Uetliberg station.

What to Know:
Planet Trail: Hike this educational trail depicting the solar system.
Summit Views: Enjoy panoramic vistas of Zurich and the Alps.

Where to Eat:
Lunch: Uto Kulm, located at the top of Uetliberg, offers stunning views and delicious Swiss fare.

Dinner: Haus Hiltl, the world's oldest vegetarian restaurant, back in Zurich.

Day 5: Water Sports and Relaxation on Lake Zurich
Cost of Spending:
Transportation: CHF 10
Activities: CHF 30 (boat rental, swimming)
Meals: CHF 60
Total: CHF 100

Getting There:
Use your Zurich Card to access public transport.

What to Know:
Stand-Up Paddleboarding: Rent a board and explore the lake.
Swimming Areas: Seebad Enge and Tiefenbrunnen are popular spots.

Where to Eat:
Lunch: Fischstube, offering fresh fish dishes with a lakeside view.
Dinner: Quai 61, for an elegant dining experience by the water.

Day 6: Day Trip to Rhine Falls
Cost of Spending:
Transportation: CHF 30 (round-trip train fare)

Attractions: CHF 10
Meals: CHF 60
Total: CHF 100

Getting There:
Take a train from Zurich HB to Schloss Laufen am Rheinfall (approx. 1 hour).

What to Know:
Rhine Falls: Europe's largest waterfall, with boat trips available.
Schloss Laufen: Visit the castle for additional viewpoints and historical context.

Where to Eat:
Lunch: Schloss Laufen Restaurant, offering views of the falls.
Dinner: Adler's Wirtshaus, a cozy spot in Zurich for traditional Swiss food.

Day 7: Parks and Gardens
Cost of Spending:
Transportation: CHF 10
Meals: CHF 50
Total: CHF 60

Getting There:
Use your Zurich Card to access public transport.

What to Know:
Zurich Botanical Garden: Explore over 15,000 plant species.
Chinese Garden: A gift from Zurich's Chinese sister city, Kunming.
Zurich Zoo: A great place to see exotic animals in naturalistic habitats.

Where to Eat:
Lunch: Parkhuus Restaurant, located in the Park Hyatt, known for its garden views and fresh cuisine.
Dinner: Kronenhalle for a final taste of Zurich's culinary delights.

This seven-day itinerary provides a well-rounded exploration of Zurich and its surrounding areas, offering a mix of cultural experiences, outdoor adventures, and gastronomic pleasures. With detailed cost estimates, transportation tips, and dining recommendations, you can plan your trip with ease and enjoy all that Zurich has to offer.

CONCLUSION

Zurich is a city that beautifully balances its rich historical heritage with a vibrant modern lifestyle. From its picturesque old town and world-class museums to the serene shores of Lake Zurich and the majestic peaks of Uetliberg, Zurich offers an unforgettable experience for every traveler. This seven-day itinerary is designed to help you uncover the many layers of Switzerland's metropolis, ensuring you make the most of your visit.

Whether you're wandering through the charming cobblestone streets of Altstadt, indulging in traditional Swiss cuisine, exploring the cultural treasures in the city's renowned museums, or embarking on scenic day trips to Lucerne and Rhine Falls, Zurich promises to captivate your senses and leave you with lasting memories.

As you immerse yourself in the unique blend of natural beauty and urban sophistication, take the time to appreciate the small moments – a leisurely coffee by the lake, a sunset view from Uetliberg, or a spontaneous conversation with a local. These experiences are what truly make a journey special.

Thank you for choosing this travel guide to accompany you on your Zurich adventure. I hope it has provided you with valuable insights and practical tips to enhance your trip. Zurich is a city that continues to inspire and enchant visitors from around the world, and I am thrilled to have been a part of your journey.

Your feedback is incredibly important to me. If you found this guide helpful, I would be grateful if you could take a few minutes to leave a review. Your thoughts and experiences will not only help me improve future editions but also assist other readers in deciding whether this book is right for them. Safe travels and enjoy every moment of your time in Zurich!

Printed in Dunstable, United Kingdom